This is MY UNTOLD STORY.

©The Life Graduate Publishing Group

No part of this book may be scanned, reproduced or distributed in any printed or electronic form without the prior permission of the author or publisher.

ABOUT THE AUTHOR

_____
_____
_____
_____
_____
_____
_____
_____
_____
_____
_____
_____
_____

Name:

Signature

This is my Untold Story

"Mother is the name for God in the lips and hearts of little children."
— William Makepeace Thackeray

The Beginning.....

Full Name at Birth
_____

Date of Birth   / /
_____

Time of Birth   :
_____

Day of the week you were born?
_____

Height at birth?
_____

Weight at birth?
_____

Place of Birth (include the City/Town, Country)
_____

Did you have any siblings when you were born? If so, what were their names and their ages?

_____

_____

_____

Add any additional notes or information here...

The Beginning.....

Share with us some information about your parents?

_____
_____
_____
_____
_____
_____

What have you been told about you as a baby?

_____
_____
_____

Did you have any unique characteristics or funny things you did as a baby?

_____
_____
_____
_____

This is my Untold Story...

Add any additional notes or information here...

The Beginning.....

What were your first words?
_____

Were you in good health as a baby?
_____
_____

Do you have any other baby memories to share?
_____
_____
_____
_____
_____
_____

This is my Untold Story...

"The influence of a mother in the lives of her children is beyond calculation."
—James E. Faust

Childhood Years

What was your favorite toy growing up?
___
___

Did you have a pet or any pets growing up?
___
___

What was your favorite T.V show to watch as a child?
___
___

Was there a moment you remember getting into big trouble as a child? Was there a punishment?
___
___
___
___

This is my Untold Story...

Add any additional notes or information here...

Childhood Years

What are your fondest memories growing up between the ages of 5 years to 12 years?

_____
_____
_____
_____
_____
_____
_____
_____
_____
_____

This is my Untold Story...

Add any additional notes or information here...

Childhood Years

Where did you grow up as a child?
(house, location, town etc)

_____
_____
_____
_____

Who was your best friend or your best friends as a child?

_____
_____

What was your favorite day of the week and why?

_____
_____
_____
_____

This is my Untold Story...

"There is no role in life that is more essential than that of motherhood."
—Elder M. Russell Ballard

Childhood Years

What was your favorite meal as a child?

_____

What elementary/primary school did you attend and where was it located?

_____

_____

Describe your most memorable moment or story from elementary/primary school.

_____

_____

_____

_____

_____

_____

_____

_____

This is my Untold Story...

Add any additional notes or information here...

Teenage Years..

Describe your dress sense and clothing as a teenager. Is there anything that stands out for you?

___

When and where did you learn to drive a vehicle?

___

What was your first vehicle and how much did you purchase it for? Tell us your special 'first car' story!

___

This is my Untold Story...

Add any additional notes or information here...

Teenage Years..

What High School did you attend and where was it located?

_____
_____
_____

Who was you favorite teacher or coach and why?

_____
_____
_____

What was your favorite subject at school?

_____
_____

Did you date anyone at High School?

_____
_____
_____
_____

This is my Untold Story...

"There is no influence so powerful as that of the mother."
—Sara Josepha Hale

Teenage Years..

What hobbies did you have as a teenager?
_____
_____

What is your most memorable moment as a teenager?
_____
_____
_____
_____
_____

If you knew what you know today, what would you have done differently as a teenager?
_____
_____
_____
_____
_____

This is my Untold Story...

Add any additional notes or information here...

Teenage Years..

Did you have a close friendship group? Have you maintained contact with any of them?

_____
_____
_____
_____

Did you have any nicknames at High School?

_____
_____

What 5 words come to mind to describe your teenage years?
1. _____
2. _____
3. _____
4. _____
5. _____

This is my Untold Story...

When I was .....

When I was a child, my mode of transport to school was..
_____
_____

When I was in my teens, the biggest news story that I recall was .....
_____
_____
_____

When I was growing up, my 3 favorite movies were:

1. _____
2. _____
3. _____

"A mother's arms are more comforting than anyone else's."
— Princess Diana

Add any additional notes or information here...

When I was .....

When I was a child, the first movie I went to the theatre to see was..

_____

When I graduated from elementary/primary school, the year was.. _____

When I was 8 years old, I wanted to be a......

_____

When I was 18 years old, my favorite music and band was..

_____

When I was in my teens, the most popular thing to do on a Saturday night was.......

_____

_____

When I was young, I loved to travel to.......

_____

_____

This is my Untold Story...

Family History

My grandparents names were:

Grandmother: _____

Grandfather: _____

They were born in: (country)
Grandmother: _____

Grandfather: _____

This is something that not many people may know about our family history......

_____
_____
_____
_____
_____

Additional Family History information:

_____
_____
_____

This is my Untold Story...

Our FAMILY TREE

Grandfather

Grandfather

Grandmother

Grandmother

Mother

Father

Me

Add any additional notes or information here...

Parenthood

How old were you when you first became a parent?
_____

Explain how you felt emotionally when you bacame a parent for the first time?

_____

_____

_____

_____

Where were you located (city/town/country) when you had your first child?

_____

_____

This is my Untold Story...

Add any additional notes or information here...

Parenthood

What has been the biggest challenge for you as a parent?

_____
_____
_____
_____

What are 3 key responsibilities you believe are important as a parent?

1 _____
_____

2 _____
_____

3 _____
_____

This is my Untold Story...

"A mother's happiness is like a beacon, lighting up the future but reflected also on the past in the guise of fond memories."
— Honore de Balzac

Parenthood

Expand on any further parenting memories you may like to share

___
___
___
___
___
___
___
___
___
___
___
___

This is my Untold Story...

"A mother's love is more beautiful than any fresh flower."
— Debasish Mridha

This is my Untold Story...

More about me!

Not many people know this about me, so let me share it with you:

_____
_____
_____
_____
_____
_____
_____
_____

The activity or hobby that I enjoy most to do now is…..

_____
_____

I have the unique ability to be able to….

_____
_____
_____

This is my Untold Story…

Add any additional notes or information here...

More about me!

If I was able to go back to a special time in history, it would be...

_____
_____
_____

If I could pass on one word of advice to others, it would be..

_____
_____
_____

There are special moments in life that you wish you could pause to enjoy for longer. Mine would be......

_____
_____
_____
_____

This is my Untold Story...

"A mother's love is everything. It is what brings a child into this world. It is what molds their entire being. When a mother sees her child in danger, she is literally capable of anything. Mothers have lifted cars off of their children and destroyed entire dynasties. A mother's love is the strongest energy known to man."
—Jamie McGuire

This is my Untold Story...

More about me!

I wish I had the opportunity to...
_____
_____
_____

The quote that resonates most with me is..

_____
_____
_____
_____

My favorite book of all time is:
_____

If there is one thing I would like to be remembered for it would be:

_____
_____
_____

This is my Untold Story...

Add any additional notes or information here...

More about me!

When I look back on my life so far, my 3 proudest moments are:

1 _____

2 _____

3 _____

If there were 3 famous people that I could invite for dinner they would be:

1 _____

2 _____

3 _____

This is my Untold Story...

Add any additional notes or information here...

More about me!

From my teen years, these are the jobs that I've had:

___

___

___

___

___

___

___

___

___

___

This is my Untold Story...

"When you look at your mother, you are looking at the purest love you will ever know."
— Mitch Albom

More about me!

One of the jobs that stands out as my most enjoyable has been..

_____

_____

The most interesting place I have ever traveled to has been…. (include the year/date this occurred)

_____

_____

_____

If I was given a free return flight to anywhere in the world, I would visit…(include your 'Why')

_____

_____

_____

_____

This is my Untold Story…

Final Notes...

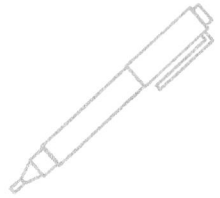

There have been many questions that I have answered in this book, but I would also like to share this with you...

Your time to write anything else you wish to share

Final Notes...

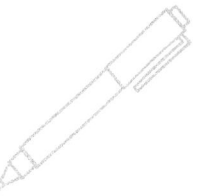

Your time to write anything else you wish to share

"If love is as sweet as a flower, then my mother is that sweet flower of love."
—Stevie Wonder

Memories

Photos, moments....anything

Memories

Photos, moments....anything

Memories

Photos, moments....anything

Memories

Photos, moments....anything